An Imperfect Life

An Imperfect Life

Poems and Drawings
by ROSEMARY OKUN

Published by
Classical Music Today, LLC

Published by
Classical Music Today, LLC
499 North Canon Dr. , Suite 201
Beverly Hills, CA 90210

Copyright ©2012 Classical Music Today, LLC
ISBN-13: 9781466225695
ISBN-10: -1466225696

Designed by Marilyn Henrion

Cover image: Ink drawing by Rosemary Okun

Artwork by Rosemary Okun

To Milt

and my loving family

ACKNOWLEDGMENTS

Special thanks to Marilyn (Mickey) Henrion, who wrote the foreword and designed this book. She is an internationally recognized fiber artist whose work is represented in museum collections. She is also my best friend and collaborator, and was instrumental in getting this project off the ground.

I am most grateful to Gerald Huckaby, my professor at Immaculate Heart College, for helping me to develop a deeper understanding of poetry and for his unwavering support, criticism, and guidance in helping me to find my voice.

Also to Garrett White from Five Ties Publishing for additional editing advice.

Also to my daughter Jennifer for her help in choosing the artworks included in this book

And to my two cats, who scattered all the poems several times during the selection process.

CONTENTS

Foreword by Marilyn Henrion

All the Years	19
Talloires 3	20
Jenny	21
At Fifty	23
Andy	25
Michael	26
Hold the Mayo	27
Three P.M.	29
Some People Satisfy	31
Mickey	32
Just Desserts	33
June Night	34
Red Riding Hood	35
Milt 3	37
Litany	38
October 9	40
Vacation	41
L'Auberge du Père Bise	42
Lists	44
I Showed Him My Poem	47
Purpose	48
Dialogue	51
Milt	52

In Memoriam	55
Our Cat is Different	56
Happy Birthday	58
I Have Been Touched by My Death	60
I Gave My Big Rug to Andy and Julia	62
Old Friends in the Village	63
Heritage	64
One Day	65
How Many Times	66
French Lesson	69
Getting Closer	70
Where Are Words	73
Insomnia	74
State of Being	76
Hollis	78
Hints for the Traveler	80
Central Park West Sunrise	82
Leaf	83
Fifty and Seventy-Seven	85
Sleep	86
Bolero	88
And What of Today	89
Dorothy in Oz	90
All Hallow's Eve	91
Humpty Dumpty	92
Dead Tree	93
Anyone for Seconds	94
Durer's World	96

Biopsy	98
Déjà Vu	99
Every Third Saturday	100
After Reading Anne Sexton	102
Ajax	103
Childhood	104
Another Christmas	105
One More Sunday	106
Only for the Trying	108
Exile	109
Born and Reborn	111
In Desperation	112
Grandpa	114
Grandma	116
Great Divide	117
I Live	119
Legionnaire	120
Old Man of the Backyard	121
Homer Goes for a Visit	122
Homer	123
I Thought of Running Away	125
I Am	126
January	127
Ice Storm	128
Certainly Not the Dog	129
Now We Are Fifty	130
Requiem	132
Faith	133

Really Rapunzel	134
Six A.M. Is	136
Rejuvenation	137
Día de Los Muertos	138
The Edwardian	139
In the Town of Trakkabaa	140
Comforter	141
I Wish	143
Nature	144
Thirteenth Gift	145
The Long Dream	146
Talloires 1	147
Bill	149
London	150
Saint's Day	151
Old People	152
Patriarch	153
Memory	154
May	155
747	156
Origins	157
Marchpane	158
November	159
Grammar	161
Process	162
Metamorphosis	163
Reader	164
Some People	166

The Glass Bead Poet   168

R's Poetica   169

The Doctor's Wife   171

Last Minute Poem   172

Thunderstorm   174

Journal   176

November Again   177

Streetscene   178

If You're So Polite Why Don't
    You Take a Taxi   181

Six Months in Solitaire   182

I Would Like   185

Life   186

October   187

FOREWORD

Born Rosemary Primont in 1928, the author grew up in a middle-class neighborhood in Queens, New York. She attended Catholic schools there until she was accepted into the prestigious The Cooper Union for the Advancement of Science and Art. Rosemary moved to Greenwich Village, where she also studied dance with Erick Hawkins. A brief marriage to a fellow student ended in divorce shortly after the birth of her first child, Jenny, in 1953.

In 1958 Rosemary met and married Milt Okun, then a junior high school music teacher, who went on to become an award-winning arranger, producer, and music publisher. Milt adopted Jenny, after which Rosemary gave birth to their son, Andy, in 1962. The Okuns have lived in Greenwich Village and Chappaqua, NY; London, England; Greenwich, Connecticut; Talloires, France; and, from 1978, Beverly Hills, California, where they currently reside.

Throughout her life Rosemary has continued to write and create art, obtaining a Master's Degree in Creative Writing at the age of fifty. She made all of the artwork in this book; until now, most of it has not been made public

Despite having traveled the world, she has never forgotten her roots and her loyalty to those who have mattered most in her life. Now Rosemary offers this legacy of one woman's inner thoughts and feelings spanning 83 years. With these poems, the author leads us with quiet grace through the hills and valleys of what she refers to as "an imperfect life."

Marilyn Henrion, 2012

ALL THE YEARS

All the years
the birds sang
outside my window
that fresh spring sound
that woke my soul
and made me glad

Woke my soul today
to childhood
sunshine mornings
when food was given
and love was mine
without asking

TALLOIRES 3

My head is ringing
avant, après, bonjour
fuddled by light wine
rouge et blanc
and incomprehensible questions
about my day, ça va

And the mountains thrust
their glory outside my window
worshipping
gris and cold the clouds
that cling

And mon fils, he waves
from the lake, over blue
and green beauty as he leaves me
for tomorrow

Et mon mari he reads
a roman he would scorn
en anglais, hélas!

JENNY

Born to October turning
red apples crisp and sweet
broad clouds soaring
smiling sky telling of children
born to visions

AT FIFTY

Smiling at the ease
of softening
at the touch
and kindness
of each other
we are
a feast
of joy and boredom
more pleasure
than trial now

Sad knowing
at the end
there will not have been
enough

ANDY

Tall boy full of promise
of the marathon
brave asking for love and giving
the child who wondered
at the moon

MICHAEL

I was wrong
I have a friend
Something I gave him
In his childhood
Never forgotten by him or me
Bound us together

It was love I gave him
Arms that held him
Spoonfuls of food
Apple juice
And a hearing ear

HOLD THE MAYO

The kids are grown
the garden is green
the dogs like everyone
and my arm pressed
against my husband
feels warm

I don't care
if the plane falls
explodes or disappears
Just let it be fast

THREE P.M.

When I came home each day
my mother met me
with arms wide open
like a great pink rose blooming
in front of the stucco house

She greeted me with apples
and vague questions about school
At her bidding I changed
into old clothes then we went
our ways till dinner

I remember
when I came home each day
my mother met me

SOME PEOPLE SATISFY

Like Milt
saving tears for the times
when only tears will help
arms that hold in a gentle way
the ones who promise
then give more

MICKEY

Her real name is Marilyn
But the kids in art school called her Mickey
Her husband sometimes calls her Mick
I'm one of the former kids
So she's Mickey to me.

It's been a long life, a shared friendship
Between two unlikely traveling companions
One the daughter of a dancing woman
From a Coney Island shtetl
The other the daughter of a dancing milkman
From an Irish Catholic shtetl in Queens

How is it that someone comes into your life
And becomes family, part of your tribe?
Fifty years of shared food and telephone calls,
Laughs, children, husbands, parents, grandchildren,
Inner lives growing, changing, pain and joy
And long months between occasional moments
Together across three thousand miles

JUST DESSERTS

I don't need to look
In the mailbox each day
For a letter that says I love you
Bruiser's worth his weight in Purina
Now that he thinks I'm his mother

He sits at my feet
While I eat
He slobbers kisses
And he looks sad when I yell
And I say
This is what I deserve

JUNE NIGHT

Pale lights
glowing cool
in the hands of children

Fill the jar
to the brim
It will not show the way

But here and there
and there in the honeysuckle
the great dark softens

RED RIDING HOOD

There were things
I wanted to say
passing through
the leaf shaded path to Grandma

About sounds
strange and beautiful
of insects, the cries of animals
and the dark woods

About sun filtering through hemlock
into child eyes
the touch of a willow
the soft moss underfoot

And about the basket of gifts
I carry
to the old woman
waiting

MILT 3

I think of him not
because he has given
me pleasure

He makes pleasure
possible

LITANY

Rose of smiles
Rose of cheerful mien
Rose of good will
Rose of happy voice
Rose of faults
Rose of feasts
Rose of loving

Rose of breadmaking
Rose of long words
Patron of pets
Patron of pots
Mistress of small mistakes
Mistress of Tai Chi

Mother of boys
Maker of poems
Rose of cheerful outlook
Rose of curling hair
Rose of deepset eyes
Rose of high cheek bones

Rose of friends
Rose of obligation
Rose of kindness
Rose of hope

Rose of pain
Rose of resignation
Rose of despair
Rose of dying
Rose

OCTOBER 9

Seven years today
and not one insight to pass on
nothing to commemorate the advent
of life without her

Though I could say she lives
in me and my children
passing through dreams
a phantom
but I know she is gone
I couldn't feel this pain
if memories were enough

And I speak of her
forcing my voice to be cheerful
who would listen if I let down
the barrier before grief

I don't think she knew
she slept
while her soft body
lost its soul

VACATION

Friends in one context
are strangers in another
a knowledge of dinner preferences
is not toothpaste understanding

Friends for years
over coffee, child pranks
and husband idiosyncrasies
eye each other carefully
sharing a towel

Time expands, demeanors
become tense and too cheerful
as two strangers
await a return to being
friends in context

L'AUBERGE DU PÈRE BISE

At ease beside the lake
coffee, books, a touch
all gifts, under plane trees
pruned for summer shade

A royal armada, the swans,
sailing towards the mountains
untroubled by thoughts of winter
or yesterday

And we smile understanding
the parting of leaves
and passing of birds
the silver sound of a spoon

And by the lake
in sunset joined
drinking from cups
with painted violets

We remember
all the years of August roses
heavy with petty angers
and share amused despair

Seeing life that might have been

had we known of September

and being still by the lake

with the swans and violets

LISTS

What can you expect of a woman
who spent years jotting down needs
on scraps of paper
carrying over one day to the next
yesterday's unfinished living

SKIRT: Take Jenny's skirt to the cleaner
she's fifteen and pretty and we fight
maybe we will love again

PRETZELS: Andy likes them
he spills crumbs on his green shirt
laughing unselfconsciously as the Captain
makes silly mistakes on F Troop

MITTENS: They're out in the snow somewhere
I must find them before dark

ASPIRIN: In this weather
someone is sure to have a headache
or catch the flu

OREOS: At forty-three
Milt sits at the kitchen table
reading, eating, listening to music
chocolate and tears, "Amor per me non ha"

SHOVEL: Jenny and I will struggle on the driveway
over how to shovel snow the right way
cheeks red, eyes sullen
neither will win

KIBBLE: For the two black dogs running in great circles
through maples and hemlocks

YARN: My mother, too old for winter,
watches from the window
waiting for us to come in
so she can give us hot cocoa
the yarn is for the white afghan she knits
thinking I will need it
to remember her by

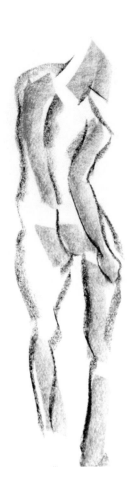

I SHOWED HIM MY POEM

I showed him my poem
the one about lists
and he said

You see I was right
There was something we had
In spite of misunderstandings
and not knowing what we were doing
that kept us together

And I could see in his face
that it made him happy
to remember

PURPOSE

One day
I filled the spoon
with applesauce
and mother bird
to nestling
put it in his mouth

remembering

skipping on gray sidewalks
learning to read
typing
and all the kisses
by the front door

and knew

that was just part of the plan
to be sure
that I would be there
to feed the baby

DIALOGUE

Where did he go when he left me
to a French class he said
I just wanted to ask him
to bring home some milk
the one in the fridge
had gone sour
the French teacher said
he wasn't there
so I jumped to conclusions
middle-aged women
jump to conclusions
he's sleeping with someone else
he doesn't love me

And just yesterday
I told my friend Carol
not to be in a hurry
to leave her husband
don't discount the years
of love and affection
as if they didn't matter

When he comes home
I will look at his face
and try to remember

MILT

My world has many colors
  taken from leaf and cave
    and the soft hissing of fear

I am Eve and the apple
  and the serpent
    and you are the garden

IN MEMORIAM

She gave me a gift
I have it in my kitchen
a folding file for recipes
food mattered

Meringues, soufflès, cassoulet
they're all in there
some in her own writing

I will give it to my daughter
and tell her not to lose it
and my mother will live
a little longer

OUR CAT IS DIFFERENT

Our cat is different
isn't that what everyone says
but it's true

We speak of cats' independence
and are piqued by their indifference
but our cat needs us

He isn't just a work of art
viewing us as signals that
food is near

That life is adequate at the moment
and there is no need to move on
to a better situation

He follows us around all day
settling by our feet, on our laps,
in our arms

When his need is particularly great
he crawls directly up our chests
two paws encircle our necks

With snakelike undulations he rubs
his seeking pleading face against
our cheeks, our ears

Trying to be part of us
wanting to chew on earlobes
nuzzle into our beings

Such importunate desire
in a human would be intolerable
but it makes us love him

HAPPY BIRTHDAY

I was destroyed by pain
the first time I saw you
and in my exhaustion
made you mine

Somewhere in those years
of watching you grow
there was so much to see
all the disjointed steps we took
and the harmonies we heard
made a pattern not known to us

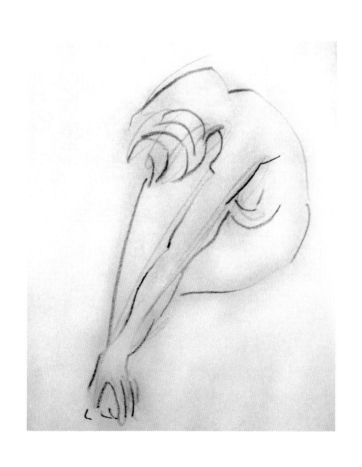

I HAVE BEEN TOUCHED BY MY DEATH

I have been touched by my death
into thinking of moments
when love breathed

The fragility of green gold
mountains in sunshine
days of summer, winter snows

Imperfect keeper wakening
to perfection
where love happened
in this second before eternity

I GAVE MY BIG RUG TO ANDY AND JULIA

After two men took the carpet to Mar Vista
from the room where it was
to the room where it is
I can breathe again

I hope the kids like it
or sell it
or give it away
and know that I love them
and I love their children

And by Thanksgiving
when we sit to eat turkey
if the rug is under their table
I'll know they will have forgiven me
for giving them that rug
because I'm too old
and tired to cope
with such a big possession

OLD FRIENDS IN THE VILLAGE

Twenty-five years is a long time
to live in Greenwich Village
not counting the years
of spiritual residence

Strollers in the hall
cold water flats, four flights up
Matisse beneath a paper lantern
and always philodendrons in a jug

Hiding for years behind dark glasses
in long skirts and sandals
a poet looking for a picket fence
with children trailing after

You know the Village
anything goes
anarchists become bureaucrats
and faithless wives are constant

HERITAGE

Willed to the child the name of one
who would have loved him had they met
Gentle man of logic joined
to a small boy obsessed by trains and planes
Wheels of the ancient engineer transmuted
to love of Thomas and Claribel

And can the love that named him Will
bring ancestral gifts to brave another century
courage that led an immigrant boy of twelve
on the voyage alone to find a new home
goodness in manhood
wisdom in old age

And what's in a name?
What other grandfathers exert their wills
in hints of smiles and cantered gaits
as swift-footed this Will runs through his time,
creating his own logic
and making sense of his world

ONE DAY

One day
I shook hands with the president
(who didn't know he shook hands
with me) and I thought
how my father would have been impressed
It was the first time in three years
of mourning
that I wished him alive

The next time
was after my mother died
I saw a couple
walking on a London street
The man was tall and stooped
and wore a gray raincoat
He was holding the arm
of a short plump woman
I didn't see their faces
but something in the way they walked
made me think for a moment
it was my father and mother
and I cried
there in the street

I must have loved him sometime

HOW MANY TIMES

How many times
have I told my listeners
the story of my life
oh, we laugh to hear the jokes
I've told, the entertaining
to a round of applause
and the sad times, bad times many
oh, we cry lightly over those
and they wring their hands with me
my listeners
tell us again they say
and I tell them
again

FRENCH LESSON

I wanted to know
the language of my ancestors
I wanted to know what they said
when they made love
and when they spoke to the neighbors
I wanted to know how
they spoke to their children
and what my great-great-grandfather said
when he stubbed his toe

But ancestry is who your mother was
and mine came from Brooklyn
with a grandmother from Syracuse
who said Glory be to God
when someone dropped a cup
and Bless me Father
when she confessed

My ancestors went by shanks mare
and shouted give him the hook
if they were displeased
They ate apple pie and
their potatoes were Idahos

GETTING CLOSER

I've returned to my twenties
and I know now what I know
I'm done with middle age
that was for finding the schoolgirl
I never was

Finished with being mother,
some stray ends to weave into wife
the hostess seems to have gone
the way of the reader,
intent on making her way to heaven
gold star for classics
blue for romance

Next the carefree teenager
I feel it coming.
will I sit dreaming over chocolates?
breakfast, lunch, dinner
lighting up my day?

And after that
the long dream before the dream.
I must hurry
and like a dog turning in downward circles
carve myself a haven

WHERE ARE WORDS

I can't find the place
where words used to come from

Maybe it wasn't a place
but a small slit, in a silken miracle
so quick that a thread of an idea
could slip through and be seen

It was my miracle, my delight
words that said I was more
than the dull being
who walked in my shoes

I made a mistake
I chose a one-person audience
and words fled leaving the page blank
and me alone in onlyness

INSOMNIA

I'm trying to sleep
But it's difficult
I was going to say it's hard
But needed a three-syllable word
Like difficult to describe the discomfort
That is insomnia

The mind that continually goes over
And over the same steps
That must be taken tomorrow
And the tomorrows after that
Starting with the first step
Each time

Me and my sprinting brain
Agreeing over and over
Repeating the planned future
A Chamberlain to a Hitler
Attempting appeasement
Capitulate and peace will come

But limbs twitch, an ache starts
And the first step repeats
Oh God, not again
Alright, so be it, again

But then to sleep
Please, this time to sleep

To sweet sleep, to dreams
To waking
Another day
Bare feet on the floor
Heart and eyes open
To tomorrow

STATE OF BEING

My stomach is full
So I guess life is good
Or should I think it's good
And ask no questions

Questions are for the hungry
And I'm not hungry
For anything
That I understand

But there is a small ache
That keeps my feet from moving
My heart covered in my chest
Dull thoughts marching slowly

HOLLIS

Remember green and white linoleum
scrubbed to sterility till we lived there
thirty years of perfection, erased in a week

Remember the apple tree outside the kitchen window
and white curtains, dotted swiss, stirring
Remember Aunt Mamie sipping tea
and Grandpa, old blind eyes and oak cane
eating eggs fried in fat, denying the pressure cooker

Remember books and radio, a green engagement ring
that was a lie, and lies that were the truth
Remember the gray car, and love the first time,
sadness and pain

Remember dreams and Gibson Girls
the Blessed Virgin
priests, prayers, and betrayal

Remember Hollis
October leaves and apples
always apples

HINTS FOR THE TRAVELER

The bartender says the Austrians are smart
they made Beethoven an Austrian
and Hitler a German, *danke schöen*

If they smiled for the Germans
and held open the doors, *guten Morgen*
it was their nature
for the English queue
Frenchmen carry long loaves
and Austrians smile, *bitte schöen*

Graceful curves along curving graceful
streets in beautiful *Wien*
and faces curved in pleasure
and all the faces
of the Holy Roman Empire passing
Mozart in the park

Neopolitans singing, Romanys selling
and the wild Spaniard on the arm
of the House of Orange
Monuments shops museums
swept and polished
sunrise to night dark, *guten Abend*

Did the now dead men smile at the Jews
now dead as they left on the trains
Does *auf wiedersehen* mean more
than just *goodbye*

And what would we have said, *good morning*
if the Germans weren't leftover enemies, *thank you,*
from a war before

Would we have held their guns
while they adjusted their helmets, *you're welcome*
and waved to the Jews
So long, fellas,
don't take any wooden nickels.

CENTRAL PARK WEST SUNRISE

Still it's the buildings
silent
always
upward prim
viewing the park

a thousand seagulls
circle
over the lake
in gray white turnings
(there was a storm)

Over up down
sky steps
Pinnacles pierce
the East River sun
The gulls are leaving

Still buildings
rise honeycombed
human alps
watching
all time

LEAF

Like leaves of a sycamore
withering to fall
I curl, enhollowing
preparing for winter
and ending

Obstacles
a breath of wind
a squirrel rushing by
and leaflike I will give up my place
and drop to earth

As inexorably as each that dies
leaving a vestige in memories
the proof of life that was
until unrecalled
I become the past

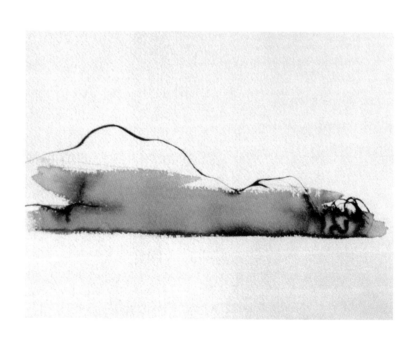

FIFTY AND SEVENTY-SEVEN

The difference between fifty and seventy-seven:
energy, oxygen, strength, balance, digestion.

I am now the exact age my mother was
when she died
I am not ready
I have things to destroy
Things to hide
Pride to pretend
As if it matters

SLEEP

Yesterday never leaves us
as we struggle for sleep
it eludes us
deliberate and sarcastic
and at the foot of the bed
ignoring our desires
for unknown reasons
naps lasting seconds
are our punishment

Soft pillow
covered, quilted
we struggle with sleep
or lack of it
my enemy

Sleep
be my friend
let me put my head on the pillow
deliver me to oblivion
to the night world that lets me love the day

BOLERO

Proud horse
pounding measured time
in stormed surf
living
grandeur of the beat
magnificent
staring
center of reason and rain
of lightning glance
black
the seeping of gold

AND WHAT OF TODAY

Early morning visit from the cat
kneading, caressing
earthy grumbling

Away animal
let me dream
of time not time
and world not world

through chambers
and fields
of my own making

DOROTHY IN OZ

On a postcard from Tokyo
cherry blossoms in the Imperial Garden
she wrote
I'm afraid to go out
everybody looks the same

She ate mustard from a small bowl
with chopsticks poised expectantly
spoke in her Nisei accent
and looked inscrutable
and not because she was oriental

Her aging blonde husband
in blue serge and black bow tie
made Brooklyn jokes
he was inscrutable too

They bought pearls and silks
and jade and laughed laughs
heavy with something
and weren't happy until they returned
to East 57th Street

ALL HALLOW'S EVE

The world would love me
if I could wear a happy mask
but the contours do not fit

Upward curves cannot be forced
upon a downturned mouth
and eyes that see

I want to wear the mask
but tears and sighs are damp
and the expression slips

HUMPTY DUMPTY

Medley of taxi
tube, elevator noise
with pilot
telling me
what state
I'm over

Not in
two weeks and ten
hours have I felt
I wasn't someplace else
than where I am

I was
I will be when I can
get me back together again

DEAD TREE

Claws of death
and dying branches
no sap flowing
no new leaves
budding green spring
against decay

I long for
mellow forest
paths worn between
ancient trees
leafed new each year

ANYONE FOR SECONDS

Why do I cook cranberries
every year
and turkey and turnips

Now that I know
how tired my mother was
when she came smiling to the table

Where are they now
voluptuous mounds
of food and flesh

Artie likes the drumstick
give grandpa the wing
more, more potatoes

And, when the red berries boil
I will act the part as if
the feast will not end

DURER'S WORLD

The woman reaches
for the child smiling
yearning for the touch
of soft hands against
her face and breast
and the trees are not indifferent

BIOPSY

When the doctor
said it wasn't cancer
Milt's face glowed
for three days

I was so far away
my place taken by the one
who doesn't feel
that I didn't know
the glow was just
love with the shades up

I remember buttercups and yellow
the back screen door peanut butter
chewing tar and the iceman
but I don't remember when
I forgot to care about living

DÉJÀ VU

Look at the girl
graduate fifty-two
more cheerful than ten
more sure than eighteen
farther-sighted
in today's glasses

Thinner lipped
grayer haired
looking straight
at the camera
as she did at three
and smiling

EVERY THIRD SATURDAY

When I was a child I went to confession
It was terrible
I knew I lied
and cheated
and had bad thoughts
but I couldn't remember
how many times
and I couldn't remember
the Confiteor

So I said
I lied five times
and had six bad thoughts
and fought with my sister
Then I mumbled the prayer
and the priest said
Say three Hail Marys
and I left in a hurry

Saturdays still keep coming
and I know I lie
and cheat
and have bad thoughts
but I'm not much interested
in confessing

I still haven't learned
the prayer
there is no priest
and I am not in a hurry

AFTER READING ANNE SEXTON

I don't want to write a love poem

singing out words of hate

I want to say that I'm alive

for a while

in a way

that I don't understand

and sometimes the green grass pleases

AJAX

A man
in the wrong place
at the wrong time
in the wrong way
a hero

Maddened
by pride
jealousy
and loathing
he hacked dumb beasts

Sane
with grief
by his own hand
on Hector's sword
he died alone

Giant
Bloody butcher
Unforgiving
God baiter
Dead hero

CHILDHOOD

They destroyed me
with their original sin
and their promises

He did
shouting and laughing
devastating drunken songs

She did
with orphan eyes
and strong arms that cried

And from the others
red-haired hatred
I disappeared

I wasn't strong
And I'm not a magician
I can't bring me back

ANOTHER CHRISTMAS

This time there's no tinsel
no treelit crèche
no plaster Christchild
It's the time between children

Breasts and beards
and hurrying hands turning pages
And we wait for new hands
to string the popcorn

ONE MORE SUNDAY

Remembering
Fights
Dislike
Things, nicked and marred

Baby prey
to a brother and sister
smarter only in age and deceit

What our parents didn't teach us
about unhappiness
priests and nuns were happy to enforce

Representatives of God they said
God's words they said everyday
and in Latin on Sunday

If you don't have faith
in the all-seeing-knowing-
everything-everywhere-God
who doesn't like human beings
there's always hell and the devil

Because
we lie and cheat and like sex
even us little ones
we steal and daydream instead of praying
and with luck, we think

So today, I'm celebrating the lack of faith
the luck that let me turn my back
on the priests and nuns, the Vatican
and the saints

But not on my parents who couldn't help themselves
and not my brother and sister
who couldn't be what they weren't
and not myself or who I am
or what I am, nicked and marred by faith
like the rest of us.

ONLY FOR THE TRYING

Does it matter how we die
if dead is dead
    Only to the dying

Does it matter how we lived
when we are not
    Only to the living

Why hope
if it is false
    Only for the trying

EXILE

King of the kitchen
knight of the parlour
disreputable behavior
throughout the house
has made the cat unwelcome

Poor Homer
now he lives outside
the windows and doors
that kept him from being
an explorer

And all day he whines
his message of rejection
through the glass
Please, Please
why me, how me, how me

BORN AND REBORN

Each time
a first time always
the only time
awakening to the past
shining
in memory a beginning
of the world
origins dreamt only
by the dreamers
with the first cry

IN DESPERATION

I bought flowers today
with my man-made money
and planted them
right in the middle of my depression

Saying to myself, a marigold
has a reason for being
that I don't know and
it doesn't know either
but sitting there red and orange
next to the delphiniums
it doesn't worry about how it failed
to be blue

Along with geraniums and pinks
and something purple
I don't know the name of
I made the world more pleasing
and if they flourish and spread
covering the bare brown dirt
I will feel I've done something good
with my life

GRANDPA

When I was a child
Grandpa looked at the switch on the wall
and said
it's a miracle, girl
you push the button
and the lights go on
just like that

He had a radio
given him by his children
on Sundays he sat in his old chair
listening to a voice from Chicago
Grandpa said,
don't touch it, girl, it's a radio.

Astronauts visit the moon
on television
not the moon outside
the one the cow jumped over
that one, flat and mysterious
shines down on my world

I laughed at Grandpa

and I laugh at me

and I laugh at my children

laughing at me

and their children laughing at them

GRANDMA

When I was born
Grandma was too old
to make new
friends

We were strangers
who sometimes met
in the hall

Grandma believed
children should be grateful
and apologize when accused

Visiting Grandma was no pleasure
for a child
who didn't like jelly bread

GREAT DIVIDE

Forget problems
Let them disappear
Think California

This isn't Maine
where life grows
in glorious green profusion

Or New York
where people scurry
in timetabled cultural activity

This is California
where it will never end

I LIVE

I live in the world of the black paint
forever waving to them across the sea
where my path is marked
in waves that lead from home

Young woman head back in expectation
belly soft the child begun
I wave hello/goodbye to their farewell
and cannot go back

My path heavy with their watching
wishing wanting in the black paint world
where I once lived
where I now live
where they still live
with me

LEGIONNAIRE

11 November 1918
I'm fine, he wrote,
The countryside is beautiful
now that the jerries have given up

Charlie and I are billeted
with an old woman and her little granddaughter
We've made a trade. I bring them food
and they teach me to parlez-vous

The old woman is a good cook
but there won't be anything
like Ma's great stuffing on Thanksgiving
Eat an extra helping for me

He was twenty-two that day
writing to his father and mother
The wonder in reading the letter
is how the nice young soldier
cheerful and generous
became the fat middle-aged bigot

But today is Armistice
And I must think well of the dead
11 November 1980

OLD MAN OF THE BACKYARD

Great misshapen tree
Who paid attention
while you grew gnarled
and threw out branches
begging for respect
and love
in spite of deformities

HOMER GOES FOR A VISIT

We packed our cat
and sent him for a visit
to the old man
who lives next door
We wanted the cat
out of the way
but he didn't know that
so he had a good time

So did the old man
He smiled when the cat
sniffed his slippers
chased a fly
chewed on a plant
and took the best spot on the couch
They had a busy day

When I picked up Homer
last evening
still dressed in his beautiful stripes
he didn't care if he never came home

HOMER

He lives with the old people now
sleeping in patterned docility
on the rust rug
Those dogs have chased him out

The old man tolerates him
The old woman doesn't see him at all
Unless someone points and then she says
"Oh"

I THOUGHT OF RUNNING AWAY

I thought of running away
of the marvelous privacy of loneliness
of eating sandwiches
when I felt like it
and drinking beer

I thought of reading until three in the morning
in bed
with the lights on
and no one
interrupting with sighs

I thought of bright sunlight coming in a window
open to the breeze
hot baths taken at leisure
time abandoned
hours of freedom

I thought of many things
and thinking
gave me pleasure

I AM

So busy packing
to leave tomorrow
I forgot
today is my life

If I think
always
this is my life
is that living

JANUARY

Silence
snow falling before noon
branches of hemlocks
bend beneath
cloud gifts

Lady needles press
to earth
graceful arms
near motionless
in the quiet gray green

A warm cover
for small living
things on earth's dry crust
grateful for respite
from the wind

ICE STORM

Listen
to the frozen orchestra tuning up
as the wind conducts
the chorus of splintered voices
tender branches falling
under the burden of beauty and cacophony

CERTAINLY NOT THE DOG

Charlie Witherspoon danced a jig
He was a happy man. Who could blame him
Not the judge who levied the fine
Not the man whose car he smashed
Not the storeowner whose window he broke
Certainly not the dog he scared shitless
The dog was in no shape to blame anybody
And the others loved the money
The judge is now known for his toughness
The man got a better car
The window was replaced by beveled glass
And the poor dog didn't have enough wits to miss
When he was up and about and trying to use them
So if there's a dog heaven
He's up there wagging his tail
Because Charlie's down here jigging
Dogs like people to be happy

NOW WE ARE FIFTY

Fifty, second half of my life,
I thought. Freedom from maternal
Dedication. I thought

Fifty. Time at the top
Not the peak of youth and energy
Not the peak of sex, I thought

But the peak of appreciation
Of sitting back to applaud
Life from a safe distance

Time to myself
Time to think. I thought
A time to wallow

Now that I'm here
I find the heights are hazardous
Not just to my own mortality

There is no safe refuge
The ancients are children
And no one knows which peak is the highest

REQUIEM

My ashes are in the earth
Me who had strong arms
Me who gave birth
Me who was child, wife, mother, widow

Do they think of me now
Do they remember my days
My arms
My pain

Have they forgotten the cold October wind
that blew over the small metal box
that contained me
when they placed me next to the man who
was my husband

His bones are in the earth
He who sang and danced
He who laughed and lied
He who was son, soldier, father, corpse

We are side by side
but we do not recognize each other
As we were in life
so we are in death

FAITH

Silent tree
full holy glowing
voices ringing
soft snow falling
I believe

Children sit
all wonder growing
staring hoping
wishful gifting

Winter maypole
dream around it
know the promise
newly born

Lost forever
saddened promise
born child none child
Hailwell Farewell
I believe

REALLY RAPUNZEL

Poor orphan, her father
left her to three virgin aunts
But she knew mothering

Possession
and plenitude
of female love
all the arts of tea
drinking kept
her company
in her ivory tower

Until the day
she let down her hair
in the arms of a prince
in a poke
wearing a salesman's smile
singing
it's a long way
to Tipperary

Nobody told her
auburn hair turns
to mouse gray thoughts
in the morning
and flesh to fat
She'd never seen a prince
before

And he grew hoarse
making excuses
Being loved by a virgin
can be difficult

And
her hands and knees
were bloody
from trying to climb
back up
the tower

SIX A.M. IS

no regrets
those are for the dark hours
of three and four
when body bones creak
long seconds on the clock
aching to unravel
sad mistakes
but six a.m.
is hope begun

REJUVENATION

Close your eyes and listen
to the mind forest
In the cool earth scent
of time rotted leaves
a squirrel scurries up
the side of a tree

Birds bend slim branches
a dust mote settles on a leaf
Is that a pebble
stirred by a snake
water dripping near the spring
Listen and be nourished

DÍA DE LOS MUERTOS

If October is
red golden leaves
a moon yellow and great

If brisk winds
brush to glowing
pumpkins smiling plump

Forget the last sad day
the sad and lost
the unspeaking
when the last leaf
clings to bare limbs
after midnight

THE EDWARDIAN

My cat lives the life
of an Edwardian dandy
wallowing in interiors
made of fine stuffs

Inventing meaningless games
to fill the time between meals
fighting mock battles
with the dog

Not for our cat
the excitement
of the chase
the cruel pleasure
of the battered mouse

Nor the freedom
of a thousand leaves
sunshine warming the beauty
of his slender frame

Yawning in ennui
he sits at the window
looking at a world
forbidden to prized possessions

IN THE TOWN OF TRAKKABAA

What happened to the little boy
who said the hole says no
What happened to the stars
that told him don't climb on the roof
What happened to green mittens
and green lollipops and the willow
that told him green stories

What happened to the moon and Jupiter
pieces of string, pink words
and the one-man baseball game
and where is the fog that had a heart and lungs
and didn't like him

Who plays one note and listens it to silence
and digs coal under the maple
and who smiles at dandelions in the green lawns
in the town of Trakkabaa
where all the trucks had wheels

COMFORTER

I'll hide your secrets
warm you in your winter nights
and days of chill loneliness
pretending I am the mother

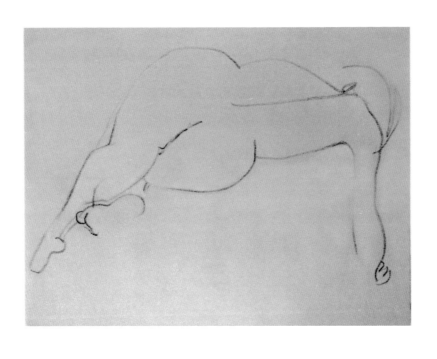

I WISH

I wish I were Emily Dickinson
marching around my garden
writing poems
with a sure touch

Not caring what happened
outside the fence
having the world
under my feet

Then happy
with my head on my own pillow

NATURE

It's the order
of things
seen and unseen
isn't it
all the green
and growing things
and things dying
and crying
real and false
and the moons
and rings
of Saturn
and pools invaded
by pebbles
and insects
and feet dancing
and fires
that burn forests
and warm nights
before the sun
calls birds
to mate
and feed
always
changing

THIRTEENTH GIFT

It's early morning
and the air smells sweet
with the scent of things
I can't name

The Greeks would have spoken
of rosy-fingered dawn
and in Britain
they still hear the dawn chorus

But Yankee grandmothers
bestow reticence

THE LONG DREAM

The cry for warm milk
in the soft breast
the strong arm clasping
lips curving in caress

The ball that flies
the song of birds
the running of hound and hare
and the fall

Into darkness and light
carrying the spirit scream
of death and desire to be
forever

TALLOIRES 1

Mist over the lake
hovering
like thoughts of beginning

Trout, curious and clever
darting from the hook
nudge amber rocks

Underwater visions
reflect deepening dawn
in the country scent
of waning August
and fading hills

BILL

I just had a lesson
with a tennis pro
who discovered Est
and forgot
that he was always good

Now he thinks
he found his center
that Werner Erhard made his stroke
but even as a kid
he could jump higher

He says
feel your power
find your space
you and the ball are on
the court for a reason

I keep my face blank
and take what works
and wonder if Est
makes being fifty
easier for the pros

LONDON

I forgot my resolution
to write each morning
that I might know
I am here

Yesterday
I must have known

SAINT'S DAY

I think today must be Saint No Word's day
because I am sitting here
inspired by his glorious gift
of nothing to say

OLD PEOPLE

In Paris
and London
and New York
I saw old people
for the first time
stepping off curbs
peering at traffic lights
clutching each other
this summer
I saw them
in my bones

PATRIARCH

A five-year-old dying
in a sixty-five-year-old body
or did he age
in the boredom
of the hospital bed

And he liked to sing and laugh
generous and nothing to give
except slippers and a pair of glasses

And the pain
we watched him
as his bones broke
there in the bed
until his long body lay still
except his lungs
grappling with time

If he had stood
where we stood looking
he would have cried out in pain and horror
at such an end

MEMORY

I thought that in music
and the fine black lines
of a moment in space
I would find life

but I don't believe it any more
than I believe
in the grand passion
of my dreaming virginity
or the divine moment
of insight
that would make me real

There is only memory
of the moments when we were
somehow somewhere

MAY

Poor May, more like
a pink day in November
gray streaking blonde
lipsticked, curlered
snaking to the candy store
feeling too sixteen

Embarrassed
by no nickels for a call
or a bus ride
and that red-faced sot
in heavy stepping blue
waving his nightstick
loving his ill temper

Poor May apologizing
for no nickels
and the ugly man
but not for the curlers

Walking down May dreams
faded blue dress dappled
in maple shade
her toothy loose smile
fluttering butterflies

747

I'm over the wing this time
poor foolish unfeathered child
whining prayers
in the chilly sunset
while the plane spreads
her bird makers
winging
her babies to roost
in the big apple

Ahhhh, no worms this time

ORIGINS

I've flown over New York
fifty times
and never known
Queens Village
was down there
over to the right

MARCHPANE

Each year we bought marzipan
shaped like strawberries and potatoes
made by the baker
whose daughter was murdered
by someone who put a red circle
on her forehead and left her
with a boy in the front seat
of a car in lover's lane

As I licked the cocoa
off the lumpy potatoes
and ate the candy leaves
stuck in the strawberries
the look in the baker's eyes
told me how my father would look
if I was murdered
but did not tell me
that the dead do not eat marzipan

NOVEMBER

Yesterday it felt like November
and I cried
for my mother dead
to all but me

November is dark
leaves withered
like the arms of my mother
sailing on the sad ship

Dead gray November
joining tears and rain

GRAMMAR

I made a big mistake
I read Dylan Thomas, T. S. Eliot
and Whatsisname
and even Whatsisname
has more to say than I
Or is it me

PROCESS

Where are poems
on days
so often now
without thought

Listing duties
distractions discontents
and omitting reasons
for living

Cell divided and disposed
ordering chaos calm
hoping, not finding
tranquility in surrender

METAMORPHOSIS

When I was one
  But I was never one
I was half of each
  Then they were me
And what I will be
  When I am not
A dandelion, a rabbit
  A hemlock

READER

Speeding through space
and tunnels of love
and otherwise

On someone else's nickel
into ecstasies of sensual deprivation
and personal detachment between paper covers

Turn out the light
before the eyes close
for the third time

SOME PEOPLE

Devour you
stealing time
with smiles
and frowns

One more request
a little one
It won't take long
Don't be selfish

Give them this day
and they
will take
tomorrow

THE GLASS BEAD POET

Thread words to wear
singing songs in clear yellow

Tell the child reds and blues
the youth rainbows reflecting the sun

Give hate dull red and brown
and opaque beads for love and worry

Green to grow in
then change to mellower tints

And make the last bead crystal

R'S POETICA

When a poem is finished
it comes out of the typewriter
into my hands
Who pushed the keys?

THE DOCTOR'S WIFE

He was leaving her
for her best friend
he said

He hadn't much time left
and he wanted to spend it
with someone he loved

They were both old
and she hadn't much
time either

So she killed him and the dog
and herself
and she didn't do it for love

LAST MINUTE POEM

What have I forgotten to do
that can be counted
against me
Are the names
the right ones
and the dates and receipts
checked and rechecked
Is everything ready
for the next one
sitting here
worrying
working up
to the last minute

THUNDERSTORM

One day I sat on the porch
with my cranky old grandmother
who scowled at the children
across the street
dancing in the rain

There were serious lightning
flashes, and gusty winds
that swirled the rain into waterfalls
around the children's faces
while Grandma clucked imprecations
at the young woman gaily
handing her drenched children
bowls to catch the rain
until the thunder became so constant
and the lightning
turned the day
to flickering brilliance

Then Grandma threw open the door
shouting You get those children inside
the young woman became sullen
(she'd heard from Grandma before)
and she pulled the children into the house

Of course, Grandma was right
no sensible woman lets her children
cavort in barefooted delirium
in the glittering green silver
of a summer morning thunderstorm

JOURNAL

A woman
who thought
she wasn't thinking

And seldom planned
who she would be
never knew

What she would say
until she said it
found herself

In realms uncharted
sitting at a typewriter
spilling words

Words, words telling
what she is. Why
is not in question

NOVEMBER AGAIN

Where are they
they were here a moment ago
whispering, sighing
sing the music
of our lives
let your blood be ours
give us tomorrow
and red apples
and burning leaves

STREETSCENE

Sometimes I'm overwhelmed by all the faces
I want to kiss and hug and stare at
all of them busy with worlds I don't know about
but they all look the same different
from me and mine and I want to tell them lets
all live now forever and never die, right here
on 51st Street where we're all hurrying away from

IF YOU'RE SO POLITE WHY DON'T YOU TAKE A TAXI

I'm going home next week to frigid toes and frozen
foreheads, red noses and a windchill factor that
will make it seem like the North Pole in a tornado
where deli means hot pastrami and a half-sour and there are
pickpockets and pockets to pick and Picasso and Johns battle
it out in the posh uptown and drunks and muggers mingle
with mothers and mailmen and bankers and poets and just
plain fakes and folks from out of town looking up and some guy
downtown fishing with a string in a subway grate

Where people roast in offices where the heat won't go off
and die where it won't go on and pipes burst and lights blink and
garbagemen strike and people get killed and married and haircuts
and deaf from the noise and oh god, I'm scared

But what can I do
It's the land of my ancestors

SIX MONTHS IN SOLITAIRE

Doing time
with the red black red
black red and all those
numbers turning up
and over promising
new starts again

I WOULD LIKE

I would like to write a great novel
crammed with intriguing ideas
devastating subplots
and fascinating people

A novel that would awe readers
by the depth of my perceptions
my grasp of life's meaninglessness
and sensuality

As I sit petting the cat and drinking coffee
I allow myself to blush modestly
At the kudos people will force on me
When I am famous

LIFE

Let the child
cross the barrier
and begin the dance
of time
begun again

Let the music
wail its dirge
in keys minor
while sun blinds the eyes
of the beholder

Let the apple be
for eating
milk the elixir
the breast
comfort

Let all forget
sad trumpets
and remember
the sweetness
of bells

OCTOBER

I'm all the thoughts
I've ever had
and all the souls of all
the flesh I've ever loved
and all the life I eat,
the people I think
the colors I dream
I am the dream
dreamt and dreaming

Self Portrait 1959

13203337R00103

Made in the USA
Charleston, SC
23 June 2012